KAPOW! Poetry & Comix
A Minizine Anthology

KAPOW! Poetry & Comix

A Minizine Anthology

edited by
Juliette Torrez

Manic D Press
San Francisco

For
Marty Kruse
and
Stephen Spyrit
in memoriam

ISBN 978-1-945665-01-1. For information, please address Manic D Press,
PO Box 410804, San Francisco, California 94141
www.manicdpress.com   Printed in Canada

CONTENTS

∞∞∞∞∞∞∞∞∞∞∞

Additional artwork:

half-title page: Scott Mills
from *Late Night Coffee and Cigarettes* by Juliette Torrez

title page & p 9: Ivan Brunetti
from *Wicked* by Juliette Torrez

copyright page: Rafael Navarro
from *The Girl with the Glass Eye* by Kenn Rodriguez

p 8: Brad Johnson
from *June Bug Melatonin* by Derrick Brown

p 160: Jordan Crane
from *My Friend Billy* by Matthew John Conley

WELCOME!

In 1998, I was working at Last Gasp, a publisher and distributor of comics, art, and literature with roots in the 1960s underground comix scene that had been one of the first to publish work by artists such as R. Crumb and Spain Rodriguez. In this wonderful world of ideas profane, provocative, and hilarious, I thought up a project matching up new work by contemporary writers and poets with artists mostly known for their work in comic books. I published my coworkers as well as friends who worked at bookstores and publishing companies, people who made zines, spoke their poetry, and created art that I found exciting or amusing. I had a twisted sense of humor—many of us did— that may be thought shocking by today's standards.

The 1990s were the heyday for zines and independent publishing. Kapow!'s first distributors were Top Shelf Books, Last Gasp, and AK Press. Indie stores like San Francisco's City Lights, Quimby's in Chicago, Powell's and Reading Frenzy in Portland, Forbidden Books in New York City, and Meltdown in Los Angeles carried Kapow! books in their zine section. The books were odd and earnest, kind of dirty, disturbing and funny.

Fifty books were intended in the Kapow! line-up; I made it to thirty. It became an unwieldy beast to keep much of the line in print while producing new titles. The borrowed Bostitch saddle stapler made it possible to create these books in a sublet bedroom I shared with James Tracy. Kapow! also fed my newly realized paper fetish as I explored vellum and cut magazines for end-pages, used fancy cardstocks for covers, and in the early days, included a Wacky Packages sticker in the back.

Contributors Janelle Hessig, Bucky Sinister, Jon Longhi, Chelsea Starr, KRK Ryden, Brad Johnson, Gabby Gamboa, and Josh Berkowitz were some of my coworkers at Last Gasp; Kevin Sampsell worked at Powell's (with Marty Kruse, RIP); Greg Zura and Scott Reynolds were on the Fantagraphics' sales team; Ivan Brunetti, Steven Weissman, and Johnny Ryan published comics with Fantagraphics; Shappy Seasholtz was working at Quimby's in Chicago; Mats Stromberg, Cara Bruce, Chuck Sperry, Lloyd Dangle, Keith Knight, Tarin Towers, and Horehound Stillpoint were running around the Bay Area;

Albuquerque tourmates Kenn Rodriguez and Matthew John Conley were brought on board...

Where are we now? Most of us, still alive (RIP George Tirado)... older, grayer, some more famous than others. David Choe cultivated a super fan base through *Giant Robot* magazine and other outlets then cashed in his stock options from a Facebook mural for millions. Ivan Brunetti, who illustrated two Kapow! books, went on to create several *New Yorker* covers, among other things. Community organizer James Tracy went on to publish four nonfiction books while co-founding the San Francisco Community Land Trust as well as the Howard Zinn Book Fair. Mats Stromberg has his own silkscreening business in San Francisco's Mission district. Johnny Ryan is making cartoons with Dave Cooper. Keith Knight has a nationally syndicated newspaper comic strip. Janelle Hessig still illustrates for *Maximum Rocknroll*. Cristin O'Keefe Aptowicz wrote a book about the Mutter Museum and married poet-turned-Hollywood screenwriter Ernie Cline. The list goes on, and admittedly, I have been terrible about keeping in touch with people. I was hiding out at a local food co-op—which really deserves its own illustrated chapbook—while these people flourished and their collective body of work amassed supernova proportions.

It is time, finally, to celebrate a weird moment in pop culture history when I was able to bring all of these wonderful people together to create a project known as Kapow!

Juliette Torrez

proof that love
makes you lie

by pleasant gehman
illustrated by janelle hessig

ODE TO TRACY HOBBS
Pleasant Gehman

She's from some planet of Amazons

via Austin, Texas

Split rail thing, sunburned,
Giant blue eyes and masses of honey hair
Face like a pioneer woman
She'd have been the one leading
the wagon train through Indian territory
Her arms are buff from carpentry
she could build a house by herself
She works on cars, drives a baby blue 1952 Packard
does plumbing
Drinks like a sailor
Swears like a Teamster
And can knot a scarf in her tangled tresses
Like a French whore

One time she showed me her pristine
circa 1963 stewardess-like slumber
partyesque make-up kit
Opened it up, and showed me its entire contents
A bolt-cutter
A bottle of Bushmill's
And a giant pinecone, from a Sequoia
Another time
In the middle of the desert
She poured me a mint julep
from a battered aluminum milk can
some of it dribbled onto her Japanese kimono
and she said, in a faux-English accent
"Why don't you kiss the hem of my dress?"
It was an honor I would have gladly paid for.

DAMN YOU, FRIDA KAHLO

by greg zura
illustrated by james kochalka

DALAI LAMA AND ME
Greg Zura

OM MANI PADME HUM
I got work backstage in a theatre
I got wood splinters on my wrists and hand
I got doors and Pellegrino for people

OM
I got to meet the Dalai Lama once
I got to shake his heavy gentle hand
I got to return his peaceful head bow
I got sight of the aura around him

MANI
I got to open the stage door for him
I got to see thousands of his followers
I got to hear the "ocean of wisdom"
I got the gist of the Buddha of Compassion

PADME
I got to clean up after everyone had gone
I got to sweep and put out the ghost light
I got to gather the "holy lord's" flowers
I got to steal lilies from the Lama

HUM
I got home to my roommate late that night
I got to explain the tenets of Buddhism
I got to tell her about peace and love
I got to give her flowers stolen from Buddha

OM
I got doe-eyed looks and light signs from her
I got touched as if I had grace in me
I got led knowingly to the bedroom
I got led knowingly to the bedroom
I got laid because of the Dalai Lama

OM MANI PADME HUM

MY LOVE

IN A PETRI DISH

by cristin o'keefe aptowicz
illustrated by josh berkowitz

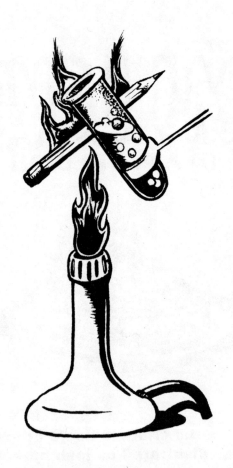

SCIENCE
Cristin O'Keefe Aptowicz

When two strands of life smash
into one another and become one
that is called fusion; cold fusion is a myth.
In order for two pieces to become one,
you need heat, a lot of it.

And there has always been a lot of heat
between us, Jason, whenever you get pedantic
and ramble on about science.

All your swan neck flasks and balding
Madame Curie, anecdotes about
Dick Feynman's van
with his own Nobel Prize winning
Feynman's diagrams
on the side, and when people would
honk their horns
and yell out their windows:

    Hey, do you know that those
    are Feynman's diagrams
    on the side of your van?

Dick would just answer back:
    Yes! I am Richard Feynman

God, I adore scientists, or maybe just you,
Jason because you will never love me
as much as you love process
    that research, hypo,
    experiment, record,
experiment, record,
conclusion, thesis,
satisfaction and contempt
that has been bred into you with every lab hour,
every NoDoz-stoned study group, every opportunity
to dig up dinosaur bones in Nova Scotia,
so you can send me a postcard covered in dust.

I wrote a poem last week swearing up and down
that I would write no more on you, no more on you,
no more on you, but this? This is not about you,
    Jason!
This is about science! This is your life choice,
this is your dream world, and I have to write
about you because you are my science,
because science is your god.

ETIQUETTE FOR EVIL

by kevin sampsell
illustrated by ivan brunetti

ETIQUETTE FOR EVIL
Kevin Sampsell

There are a few things you should know about The Devil when he enters your home.

First: He wears no shoes and his socks are often filthy and/or torn.

Second: He likes your mouth, and frequently will try to put his hand inside it.

Third: He is an emotional wreck. Do not let him touch the wine and do not probe too deeply with your questions.

He likes fried foods. Shrimp is his favorite. He'll eat your leftover tails too. He says they feel like helicopter blades in his throat. For a beverage, have plenty of Dr. Pepper on hand. He loves that stuff, and not just because he owns the soul of the man who invented it.

He will talk a lot while eating and he says the word "soul" too often for your comfort. You may ask him bluntly what he does with these souls when he has them signed over to his name.

"I arrange them in my living room and watch TV with them," he explains. "I have conversations and arguments with them. They are just like the friends you have that visit you. But when I get bored I can stretch them out and bounce on them like trampolines."

You may notice that The Devil likes to play with ice cubes in his mouth before spitting them across the room. He also bites his nails while releasing tiny, poisonous farts. Humor him when he does these things by giggling timidly and remember to constantly remind him that he is pure evil.

If you are going to a movie, keep in mind that he does not like Mickey Rourke or Richard Gere.

He will pay for your ticket and he will buy popcorn with extra butter and salt. He will offer his arm as you walk down the aisle. He will want to sit close to a fire exit because it makes him feel at home. When the lights go low, he will put his long arm around your shoulder and pull you close to him. You will feel his hot breath exhaling from his flaring nostrils. When you are relaxed, he will stick his hand in your mouth.

When the evening is coming to a close you must be firm yet friendly.

He may wish to "come inside" for a nightcap or hot espresso drink. He is not above pleading, and is known to complain during these moments about his feet. Avert your eyes from the dirty socks. Maybe offer to buy him shoes on your "next date." Don't say sandals. He will explode in anger if you say sandals. He will wake up the neighborhood if you even slightly suggest that he wear sandals. When The Devil thinks of sandals he thinks of machine guns. Do not say sandals at any time during the evening and avoid wearing them yourself.

While we're on the subject, I should also point out that The Devil's facial hair is called a "Goatee" and not a beard. "Beard" is also a bad word to utter in his presence. He likes the word goatee and explains that Christians find the term "creepy." So never say "beard" unless you want to deal with 911.

It is important to maintain control of these last moments of your date. It is fun to date The Prince of Darkness, or at least not boring, but if you let him manipulate you on the first date he will never develop deep, caring feelings for you and will dump you like a month-old angel food cake.

Purse your lips tightly closed and kiss him tightly on his lips. Watch for his hands—they could gravitate toward your mouth for one last aggressive attempt at entering. Compliment him and tell him you'll be excited to see him again, perhaps next Saturday night. He likes to sleep in on Sundays.

H.R.

**by kristen casselman
illustrated by lloyd dangle**

HR 3
Kristen Casselman

i want
i really really want
warm berry pie
served on the stomach
of Henry Rollins
à la mode
no plate

i want
i really, really want
to nip at his ice cold nipples
and floss sticky sweet chest hair
through my front teeth

i want breasts that don't sag
joints that don't ache
and sex i don't have to plug in

i want one full day without being condescended to
without being treated like
an idiot because i don't have a penis
and don't want one

one full day where
i'm not patted on the head
and stabbed in the back

i want to win the lottery
kiss my day job goodbye
finish my novel
and pick up my Pulitzer

and i want
i really, really want
Henry to read me Cohen
while rubbing my feet
and feeding me mangoes
i don't think it's too much to ask

It's Times Like These

by mike henry
illustrated by eric reynolds

MY GRANDPARENTS HAD CHICKENS
Mike Henry

A small shack behind their red brick
Norman Rockwell-esque home
housing dozens of small, bitchy birds
packing and clucking and stinking
that mealy acrid stink.

I remember how the first time I smelled
the fevered sweat of a friend on crack
that the scent slingshotted me back
to that chicken coop, shoveling feed for the flock.
My tanned forearms showed scars
from scratches and pecks in the war for eggs,
commerce and kidnapping
played out like Shakespearean tragedy.
I sang to the birds because Grandma told me it
would help. And when it didn't
I cussed at them, these maddening pigeons
from hell, wondered why they never figured out
that if they actually took a run at it and
flapped like fuck that they could clear
the chain link fence, the braided metal wall
with a symbol of a dog on the gate signifying the
small collie named Lady that
chased the chickens around the yard,
tirelessly, joyfully. I quickly realized that
they wouldn't have anywhere to go. Better to stay,
play the odds against a batter-fried end
in a cast iron skillet.

It was many years later that I would learn
that the chickens were sort of a leftover.
That before the red brick mountain stood that had
always been Grandma's house to me, there was
a small, ramshackle building
made of plywood scraps
and tarpaper leaning bravely into the stinging wind.
That the family had lived in a shack, more or less
an exaggerated version of the chicken coop
out back.

As a grown man, 30 years of age, I finally
hear stories of how my father was afraid to take
his soon-to-be-bride, my eventual mother,
home to meet his folks.

Mom took it bad,
thought Dad was embarrassed,
that she was too fat.
Truth was that there was no running water inside
and my Grandma's head shook softly in apology
that she never coulda done better by her boys.

See, there were patches of floor where there was
no floor. The packed earth hid under thin squares
of mismatched carpet samples
discarded by Woolworth's.

Even a mother's love
cannot make alchemy
from threadbare second-hand furniture
with cinderblock legs,
or shine away the brown scars
burned by her husband's forgotten cigarettes.

See, Dad was the youngest of five brothers,
years of quiet pride set into his jutting chin.
Dad was protecting secrets of a poor
Oklahoma family, the same secrets that
steeled his thin arms and legs to strength,
partly from fights in alleys defending
the family name against white-trash
name calling, partly from chasing chickens
around the yard, carrying away their eggs
as if they were hushed voices
speaking songs.

merry christmas, jewboy

by dayvid figler
illustrated by pete sickman-garner

MERRY CHRISTMAS, JEWBOY
Dayvid Figler

Trim? Trim?

Thank you—no.

Need to get away from your tree
with ornaments sparkling like
miniature golden calves
gleefully awaiting a-milkin'.

During the afternoon
it silently
screams in your living room
in front of the television set left on
    the Maury Povich show.

(Help me)

For every tree you pluck
from the Mother's womb for sacrifice
I plant an olive
in Israel

"A-ha!" you scream, "Scrooge Jew!"

But I have absolutely no desire
    to bash your Jesus Christ
(if he even existed)
I actually like your Christmas,
some parts
just seem
a little
wrong.

The Rankin/Bass puppetronic
television specials seem a little wrong.

Rudolph the Red-Nose Reindeer may be fiction
but the story leaves
    gingerbread crumbs of morality in
the corners of children's sleepy eyes.
What lessons are to be learned
when the other reindeer only accept Rudolph
after Santa showed an interest in him
and Santa only intervened
when the foggy chips were desperately down?

Rat bastard reindeer!
Let him play your games,
it's not like he wants to copy your test or
join your fraternity or
move into your neighborhood.

And that shiny nose
Not just like a light bulb
But an actual light bulb
Is he bionic?

The only other representation
of a mammal with a red light bulb for a
nose is the patient in the
game, Operation, which is
made by the unholy
makers of Ouija boards

This alleged "game"
encourages children to vivisect a living
human specimen without
the benefit of even a local anesthetic

(Pulling a funny bone from a live man
                    —that isn't funny.)

There are death berries
in the middle of mistletoe, yet underneath
them you open mouth kiss?
There are people starving next door, yet
string popcorn for decoration?

It all comes back to that tree
A sweet angel as a cherry on top
(Is she a voice from the other side?)

Celebrate peace, joy, and love,
I have no quarrel with your faith.
I respect yours as I hope you respect mine
Go heartily and Hallmark your calendars.
Find boughs
upon boughs of holly and
deck deck deck
Sing the praises of your Virgin Mary
and your Virgin Joseph, too (think about it)

And me?
On Christmas day,
I will open my eyes
head to the mailbox
and simply wonder
why the postal service has
forsaken me.

by noel franklin
illustrated by krk ryden

THEO
Noel Franklin

what do you call a drummer without a girlfriend?

homeless

he says
and all smiles saturate with beer and biting irony
there being truth in that
i mean, how many girls do you see
waving their lovers off to work
while they sit content in their practice spaces
"johnny's gone, girls!
let's get out the sticks and picks and distortion pedals!"
i'm not even in a band
i just do paintings
but we're all short of support, time, materials
all wishing we had rich relatives, like vincent van gogh
his life was not easy
still, if he needed anything to keep painting
he just wrote his brother
he wrote

"dear theo, send more yellow."

of course!
but i have no well-off family
or drummer boy
with a garage practice slash studio space place to be
no, i've got one of those high paying jobs
that women work out of desperation
i've got the body for it and the gear
i just move through rooms densely populated with men
wielding my power tool of choice
in this case
a welding lead
because i am a welder
that's what i do for a living
long hours spent in shop or shipyard
playing rosie the riveter to a modern day military
before crawling home to dream heavy dream
of welding, again
except this time i am arcing billboard size letters
until the entire naval refueler starboard side reads

"dear theo, send more yellow."

except the yellow never comes
i am losing track of what van gogh must have been seeing
the sky over seattle is starless and flat
raining a drizzle of gray over everything
my vision gray, my canvas gray
my whole world gray
enough
to actually consider one of those desperate jobs
putting my mind on hold and body on lease
but when i imagine myself as a dancer
the image i conjure
is me, in my welding leathers
stomping my boots on the foot of the stage yelling

"dear theo, send more yellow!
dear theo, send more yellow!"

and the men
who pack razzmatazz or deja vu or the lusty lady
they say
"we understand
you don't have a brother
who sends you money for your paintings"
so they start a collection
write checks for a trust fund
have me to dinner with their families one night a week
there's drinks on the house
the doors are thrown open
the room fills with sunlight and smiling cacophony
women and children start filing in
each one with instruments
it's like the whole seattle band scene starts playing
with full orchestra
and the odd homeless drummer
the welders serenade secretaries
and i am living a version of *it's a wonderful life*
still in my leathers
blissfully crowd surfing
held by hands, hearts
voices, unison, chanting

"dear theo, send more yellow"

MY Friend BILLY

by matthew john conley
illustrated by jordan crane

PINK
Matthew John Conley

The cotton candy center
spins outward around the walls of the carnival
her pink sweater pulls at my arms
as we dance through the catcalls
at closing time,
the blue sky drains down into her eyes
& her blond hair rises off her shoulders
& interweaves w/ the stands of cotton candy
that wall us in so sweetly
as we dance through the carnival
just before it closes

& you I say
you are sweeter than the whole round world I say,
& she smiles w/ big round sex swirling down
below her throats, & the sun & moon turn
& spin in amongst the strands of cotton candy
that wall us in so sweetly
& the whole wide sky is turning pink in her sweater
& we line our stomachs with cotton candy
as we dance through the carnival
just before it closes.

WEIRD BOB

by chelsea starr
illustrated by johnny ryan

WEIRD BOB
Chelsea Starr

Weird Bob was a tall gangly speed freak who was always darting around the neighborhood on these weirdo bikes he made from bits and pieces he stole from other people's bikes. His B.O. was strongest anyone had ever smelled. It was the kind of B.O. that chokes the air right out of you in order to make more room for itself. It was so big that it became this thing that, while still strongly associated with Weird Bob, became its own separate entity. Like a stinky ghost that followed Weird Bob and hung in his wake.

Weird Bob's girlfriend Margie May was a skinny stringy-haired hippie chick who was actually pretty in her own way. No one could ever understand what on earth she was doing with Weird Bob. Margie's sister Izi lived next door to us and was lots older than Margie. And she was freaky. I remember when we first moved into that house, she and her husband came over and wanted use to let them in so they could see our basement because Izi had all these horrible dreams about it and her husband thought if she could just SEE it, she'd realize there was nothing to be scared· of. My mom wasn't home and my sister and I didn't know what to do when they pushed past us and descended into our dungeo-nous new basement. So we followed then down the stairs just in time to witness Izi's Grand Freak-Out.

She screamed and chanted and her eyes rolled back in her head. "It's just like I knew it was!" She cried, "This is IT!"

"Those shelves," she said, gesturing to the crudely constructed wooden shelves that lined a wall of the unfin-ished basement. "Those which are now home to cobwebs and mouse droppings... were once home to jars."

She paused dramatically. "Jars," she said again, "of human hearts and livers." That said, she recommenced her screaming and carrying on and was up the stairs and out of the house in a flash, leaving my sister and brothers and I to have our own Grand Freak-Out.

The winter their baby came, Weird Bob and Margie May were living in the green tin tool shed is Izi's backyard. Izi's house was plenty big for them to have slept inside, but Weird Bob was not allowed in the house because Izi was convinced he was an archenemy and a vampire. And so, if Weird Bob could not set foot in Izi's house, neither could Margie because the two were very much in love and one in solidarity and because Bob said he would kill Izi if Margie forsook him for her.

When it was December and Margie was eight-and-a-half month's pregnant, Weird Bob disappeared for a while to be reunited with his other true love: the carnival. He was a self-proclaimed expert at working the tilt-a-whirl and couldn't be kept away from it for too long or he would just die. He wanted to take Margie May with him, he really did, but he said there's no place in the carnival for a woman, especially a pregnant one. So, then Margie was living out in the shed without even Weird Bob to keep her warm. She still couldn't even stay in her sister's house because she was afraid that Weird Bob would come back unannounced and kill Izi. One day my mom, who has always had a heart for pregnant homeless women in need, saw Margie wandering around aimlessly in the snow, blue-lipped and disoriented. So she wrapped a blanket around her and said she should come stay with us for a while.

Margie moved in and before we knew it, Weird Bob had rolled back into town and set up camp in our basement. My mom wanted to kick him out, especially after he set up his meth lab in the corner of the basement that my mom said was too near the dryer, but she knew if she'd made him leave he'd carry out bizarre retaliatory acts against her. Besides, she didn't want Margie and her unborn baby girl freezing to death out in the shed. So she let him stay. And actually it turned out to be kinda good for everyone involved because with a new on-site meth lab, my mom didn't have to buy her drugs anymore, thus freeing up extra funds to be spent on things like oil for the furnace.

So when the house was warm and when my mom would leave for a few days here or there, Bob would take certain liberties like turning up the furnace up to ninety degrees and sauntering around the house in cutoff jean shorts that were so disgustingly short that his hairy schlong hung out the bottom. "Don't be scared—he's just saying hello," he'd say to my sister and me as we tried not to look at it. "It's natural."

"No," I said, "it is NOT natural. It isn't one bit natural to have a fucked up carnie making pot brownies in your kitchen with his big hairy schlong hanging out." But Bob gave me a brownie and it made me think, maybe it was natural. Maybe I was a prude like boys at school said, and maybe this is what people did—walk around with their big hairy schlongs hanging out... and maybe you're not supposed to want to puke at the sight of them.

Sometimes things were nice. I remember one time Bob came into a few bucks just in time for a special they were having at Domino's Pizza, and he bought each of us kids our very own pie. We all went nuts, of course, eating every last scrap all at once and then puking one by one in quick succession. Bob thought that was pretty funny. "Avoid the Noid," he kept saying. "Avoid the Noid!"

Things turned cold, so cold, when the baby—named Suzy Q—was about two months old. Weird Bob has squandered so much oil pretending the house was the tropics that the furnace was dry and the house was an igloo. We kids were all very cold and resentful. My mom was mad at Bob for turning her kids into potheads. Bob was mad because the baby took up so much of Margie's attention. Margie was mad at everybody for being so mad when there was her lovely Suzy Q to gaze upon.

Luckily, though, just as the tension in the house was at its all time height and Bob's B.O. was at its all time enormity, Margie's name was drawn at the H.U.D. office and they were getting squeezed into a little mini-project over on Jefferson by the library.

"Perfect," Margie said. She liked to read.

**by tarin towers
illustrated by ron rege jr.**

AMERICAN HERITAGE
Tarin Towers

She skipped tenth grade
And didn't get laid till she was twenty.
She thought this was pretty funny
Until it happened, and then Fuck!
She said, for the first time knowing
What David Bittner said he knew in the first place.

The wooden condoms started making sense
And so did French, those sleazy vowels.
She saw herself as rotted and immense
A tracking dog, with fewer brains than bowels.
So she pressed up her face against the glass
And addressed, assessed her future as
    a piece of ass.

by cas mcgee
illustrated by keith knight

IMANI, *for Darren*
Cas McGee

you are hopeless
the way you remember
we called each other "cuz"
even though we weren't blood
related only 'cause
our kinfolk came up together
around Pontchartrain Park
along Campus Blvd.
and had neighborhood nicknames like
K-Boy, Ricky-T, Fathead
Pistol, Tick, and Spook
they owned the block
marked street corners as turf
I still have the stop sign
my Uncle Kevin boosted
from the corner of Press & Pressburg
man, we never did cool shit like that
we didn't even have neighborhood nicknames

you are hopeless, Darren
it was bad enough back in high school
you were the only brother I knew—
who was into The Cure
don't get me wrong
I had my own things going on
with XTC
Oranges & Lemons
and that damn *Skylarking* album
playing "Dear God" just low enough
that I wasn't accused of blasphemy
I must've blasted "Ballet for a Rainy Day"
about a million times
but, damn, at least I played some Black music
some Black boy lost is what they called you
some Black Boy lost and
standing on a beach with a gun in his hand
staring at the sea
staring at the sand
staring at the stark whiteness
    of Robert Smith's face
trying to find himself

you are hopeless, Darren
growing dreadlocks
apparently you are shell-shocked
from epic battles you had with
mind-altering substances
yours was a mind better left alone
months of living
or as you say
dying in an institution
left you paranoid and unsure
of the world's intentions

you only crumble herb now
'cause everything else just makes you crazy
but you're freaking me out
and the fellas with that talk of
how the doctors messed up your mind
and about the ill effects of smoking shrooms
I don't know much about the doctors
but I do know
you don't smoke shrooms, bruh

you are hopeless, Darren
growing dreadlocks and changing your name
so your parents give you grief
what else is new
so you're misunderstood
join the club

so institutional experiments left you bent
well, you're free now
but you won't be if you keep acting like some
crazy nigga
that's what they call you now
some crazy nigga
some crazy nigga growing dreadlocks
some crazy nigga growing dreadlocks
    and changing his name
some crazy nigga growing dreadlocks
    and changing his
    name to Imani

Imani
is that going to make things better for you?
Imani
is that going to change your life?
Imani
is that your neighborhood nickname now?

what does it mean?

faith
Imani means faith

LAST NIGHT I DREAMED OF ANGELS

by george tirado
illustrated by jaime crespo

ANGELS
George Tirado

martin luther king once said "i have a dream"
so did i   you see i dreamed in techno
blood red and 415 blue   cuz you see

last night i dreamed of angels
angels

in the early morning tenderloin crack crawls
with split lips and blackened eye and broken
wings hoping that this next hit might
make her fly

last night i dreamed of angels
angels

dirty young man smelling of cheap cisco wine he
removes his clothing and steps away from his
cart then does a drunk tai chi dance naked
in front of god and all the laughing masses

last night i dreamed of angels
angels

a tired old man with yellow stained fingers
dirty face snot on beard
he hands me his last twenty without
looking down rounds the corner then he's gone

last night i dreamed of angels
angels

youngsters tagging sagging
and flagging great walls
with encryptions only they can read but put there
unto death

last night i dreamed of angels
angels
angels
angels
floating
falling and drifting
angelic prostitutes dressed in torn red silk
falling
spiraling
floating
they reach for their date which is death
he is dressed in a red tuxedo he hands them
a dead red rose wrapped in a red ribbon
tonight they will cry and hold him close
and never let him go
tonight he will laugh and not let them stumble
floating
dreaming
on celestial dream music

last night i dreamed of angels

JUNE BUG MELATONIN

by derrick brown
illustrated by brad johnson

MY RUSSIAN JEWEL
Derrick Brown

My hands turn to Sue Bee honey
and my nails flip over to reveal
        pink crescent moons
when i think of our first night together.
Will it be like a tornado or sheets,
or timed with the cadence of drooling candles
and the bass of pile drivers?

Wild enough to embarrass the furniture
Woman girl, I want to hold you
the way grasshoppers hold onto their bows
the way sand creatures hold down sailors' bodies
the way children hold onto pennies and secrets.

Is it fair to say I might not have love with you
        on honeymoon night?
Cause I might be sore from doing it with you
        all day
in the train,
under the reception table
in every public restroom we stop at
from here through all of our North America
...cause I'm kinda romantic.

So instead, that night, we'll just have to sit there
speak about the pieces of electrical tape we ever slept with
and wish we had never touched anyone else.

the girl with the glass eye

by kenn rodriguez
illustrated by rafael navarro

ROOMMATE
Kenn Rodriguez

he never does, he never does
he never does the dishes
he never does the dishes 'cause
he's always in his fucking room
& the big steak knife is always missing
when we go and try to cook something
& the big pots and pans are always missing
when we go and try to cook something
& the guys and girls who stand on the corner
a block away from my house
are always missing
'cause he never does the dishes
he never does the dishes
& he's always leaving the house
after midnight
he's always leaving the house after midnight
with trash bags and shovels
he's always leaving hair in the sink
I think it's his
he has so many different colors on his head
& he's always leaving
with the boys who stand in the park
& the girls who stand on the corner
a block away from my house

& the talking head on the tv news
is talking about the
gay boys & gay girls
& homeless boys & homeless girls
who stand on street corners
& in the park a block away from my house
always go missing
but my roommate,
he never watches the tv news
he never watches the tv news
and he never ever does the dishes

by cara bruce
illustrated by mats

AUTO EROTIC
Cara Bruce

Careening down the hill, clinging
tightly to every curve, the car's
wheels screeched in mechanistic horrors
I could picture the occupants—their
skin stretching smooth with the speed
tightening against their pounding skulls

I could almost feel their bowel-contracting,
pants-pissing,
handshaking, pure delicious
panic.

Sitting back, I took another swing of
my beer, my tongue slipping out
to lick thick traces of foam off my
lips. I put the beer down and picked
up the binoculars. The driver had
almost lost it on the last turn but,
unfortunately, seemed to have
regained control.

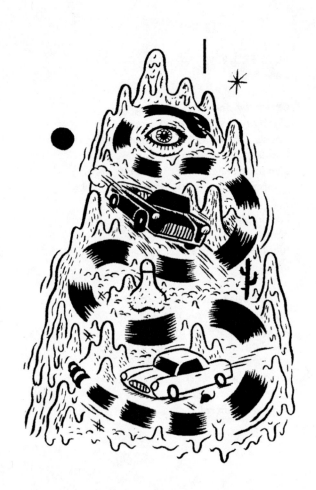

My pulse was raging. It wasn't often
an asshole came this close to
crashing. He had me hot-aroused
and steaming. If he made it down
alive, got me this close without the
payoff, I'd run down the hill and kill
him myself.

Right hand down my pants, I mindlessly
rubbed my clit in repetitive
circles, but the edge was off. The
fucking bastards were probably going
to make it after all. I put the binoculars
down and looked around. I was
alone on a cliff overlooking the San
Marino freeway.

The black asphalt of the road was
laid over hairpin turns like skin
on a slithering snake. The rocks
mirrored the ones behind me, a
jumbled mess of colored graffiti
staining their surface.

The scream of the tires jolted me
and I lifted my binoculars just in
time to see the car plunge tightly
into the final turn. Tight, but not
tight enough. Shooting off the road,
the car caught the side rail and
started to roll, bouncing form rock
to rock.

Moving my hand faster and faster
against my sizzling, swollen clit,
I watched the car bang from one
sharp crest to the next, flipping tail
over nose, circling, twirling until it
landed, shaking, quivering—then
finally still.

Inside, I knew they would be
haphazardly splayed in the wreckage,
human abstracts with necks snapped
in impossible angles, faces crushed
and embedded with glass, jagged
slivers slicing flesh and arteries, their
blood pooling on the leather seats. I
came so hard I bit my lower lips and
tasted my own metallic blood.

I lay back against the rock and
waited, licking the pussy juice
from my fingers and washing the
blood-taste down my throat as
police sirens started ringing in my ears.

SENSITIVE LITTLE POETRY BOY

by shappy
illustrated by sam henderson

SENSITIVE LITTLE POETRY BOY
Shappy

Oooooooooooooh!
Listen to me!
I'm a sensitive little poetry boy
Nobody likes me.
Maybe because I'm too
in—yer—mutherfucking—face
MUTHAFUCKA!
OR-maybe-because-I-breathe-in-between-every-word-I-say.
Or maybe I shock you
with my darkest sexual secrets.
Like how my mother would
put her cigarette out on my gonads
and still does
every time I go home for Christmas?
Oh lord, please!
Please listen to the pathetic little poetry boy!
You can see me at every open mic
I'll be sitting in the back...
brooding.
I read the same two poems I read every week.
Hey, I only wrote them two years ago
and they're both about my ex-girlfriend
from five years ago, well, actually
she wasn't technically my girlfriend.

I was stalking her or at least
that's what her lawyers say,
I'm totally over her... wait, is that her?
Across the street?
Oh, my... wait, it's just a mailbox
And no, I don't slam! The so-called poetry slam
has nothing to do with poetry.
Not real poetry! And no, just because
I got booed off stage
has nothing to do with it!
Cuz I'm a real poet.
With real emotions
and real tears
and real shitty poetry
so fuck off!
You don't fucking get it!
Get the fuck outta here!
Wait, before you go can I read you this poem
about how much I want to fuck you?
I'm sorry, I mean, make sweet poetic love to you?
Because I'm a candy-ass-please-
don't-kick-my-ass Nancy boy.
I'm a lonely, insignificant, sensitive
little poetry boy and my notebook
is only half full.
God help me.
God help us all.

EVERYONE AT THE FUNERAL WAS SLAMDANCING

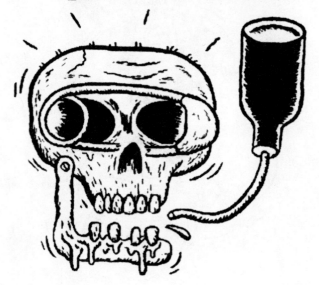

by jon longhi
illustrated by mats!?

EVERYONE AT THE FUNERAL WAS SLAM DANCING
Jon Longhi

It's the sound of hammers drumming that
wakes me up from a long coma in the dream.
But when I come to my senses, I realize it's
actually the rhythm of pallbearers nailing me
into my coffin. I scream and yell and pound
on the velvet roof of the casket but they
can't tell my fists from the hammers because
I'm keeping the same beat. I worry that two
nails will go right through my palms. And no
one can hear my screams over all the loud
punk rock music they're playing at the
funeral. Teenage skaters are doing skateboard
tricks on my coffin while the priest
reads my eulogy. Most of the mourners are
slam dancing. Everyone is drunk.

DONUT HOLE

by james tracy
illustrated by gabby gamboa

MINUTEMAN
James Tracy
(for d. boon)

minuteman!
minuteman!
minuteman!

i dreamt i saw d. boon playing
woody guthrie's guitar,
the one that said
"this machine kills fascists."

not all great revolutionary guitarists
are killed by fascists

(sometimes they are killed by car crashes)

before they get a chance to kill one.

the moon over tucson is forever sad

minuteman!

Yespants

by greg gillam
illustrated by kevin scalzo

VOCABULARY EXERCISE
Greg Gillam

I'm hosting this poetry reading and I want to be ultra-positive, give the performers lots of affirmation. So I make this suit covered with the word "Yes."

After the show I'm hanging out with the poets, contemplating big issues such as, "Someone I like is here, will they notice I'm interested?"

An inner voice answers, "Well, of course. You've got 'Yes' all over your pants.

And it hits me—a new word. Yespants.

Now years ago I saw an incident which illustrated this word.

I lived by Paris nightclub, the best-known lesbian bar in Chicago. Not due to quality or identity, but because it was the rare Chicago bar with a full parking lot.

It was a Spring night. Spring is an interesting time in Chicago. After prolonged cold we forget the outdoors is not just another large living room, and our Midwestern reserve is dropped for ornate public emotion.

So I'm strolling past Paris and this couple is having a huge fight in the parking lot. They are breaking up, in fact, and it's clear why.

One woman is in a business suit, like she just got off work. She's shouting at her future ex: "Just stepping out? I'm not a moron, I'm not a dipshit. If you're just 'stepping out,' why are you wearing the same jeans you had on the first time you slept with me?"

I looked at the jeans: red denim bell bottoms that went from a wide cuff to thigh hugging, waistband so low on the hips she must've had spirit gum on her pelvis to keep them on. Jeans to get any girl to go home with you. Yespants if I ever saw them.

Miss Yespants was not happy with the situation. Rules she meant to bend were broken.

At the time, I had no term to describe the scene except "BUSTED." Now I've got a better one: Gettin' caught with your Yespants on.

We've all got Yespants, no matter what your preference or shape. They don't have to be tight, just encase the crotch in a way that indicates availability. They hug or hang or shimmer with something that sez, "mmm-hmm." For some they are shorts—the short shorts boys wear on Halsted Street during Market Days are "you betcha" pants. Skirts, the underwear seen beneath them—those can be Yespants.

Some people wear nothing but Yespants. Be careful of them. Careful with those Yespants when you're going steady. Don't say you'll be home and then wear them out. 'Cause then...

Later that same night, I was in a diner when the woman in the suit came in. She knows I was a witness, the senses of the betrayed are heightened.

"It's over," she told me.

"That sucks," I said.

"What the fuck is that shit?" she asked.

"Yeah, that shit is fucked up," I reply.

"It's just such fucking shit," she cried.

And so we went on, conjugating 'shit' and 'fuck.' Had I known my new term back then I could have said:

"You caught her in Yespants. I'm so sorry."

And instead of merely swearing in that parking lot, she could have worked the poetry, saying:

Girl
I caught you in your Yespants
I know them well

Remember that first morning
they were pooled among my sheets
red denim like spilled blood
from a pact that made my blood into yours

And when you moved in
I said do what you want
with the rest of your wardrobe

Those pastel skirts
you wear to work at the flower shop
rubbing thighs
as you finger roses
and discuss the latest Supreme Court decision
I care not

But your Yespants
the slacks that say "oui"
they belonged to me

Now? Take them

Take the pantalones que dice "si senorita"
and wear the motherfuckers out
for all I care

But realize
when you get home
the locks
may say "no"

**by bucky sinister
illustrated by kurt wolfgang**

SOUTH BOSTON, NORTH HELL
Bucky Sinister

I was somewhere in Boston
getting my ass kicked by Catholics again
hockey style,
where they pull your coat over your head
so your arms are stuck
while they hit you.

At that moment
I imagined
my friends in Arkansas
were getting drunk
losing their virginity
and wrecking hot rods
while I was taking a beating
for something I wouldn't even believe in two
years from then.

I had pissed off some Southie kids
by inviting them to church.
Everyone in our church
was supposed to ask strangers on the street
on a daily basis
to study the bible with them.
Being 15 years old, this kind of response
was all too common.

These kids liked to fight,
fistfighting either
like boxers
or hockey players.

When you've been beaten up enough times
your body learns how to go numb on the first hit.
After that you hear the punches
more so than feeling them.
It sounds like dribbling by yourself in a gym
cannon shot echoes
bouncing off the loneliness of your ribcage.

I was taking a beating
that would leave me with permanent hearing damage

I was taking a beating for Jesus
turning the other cheek
the other eye
the other lip

I was taking a beating
one in a series of many
and each time
I wanted to be anywhere else
but there was nothing I could do
except listen to the rhythmic pounding
and look down the long tunnel
of my coat.

All I could see
was a small circle
like a searchlight
showing me sidewalk
cigarette butts
and sneakers
while I looked for some friendly piece of
ground
I would never find.

by horehound stillpoint
illustrated by krk ryden

REINCARNATION WOES
Horehound Stillpoint

in my other life
I am a Ninja villain
with dagger for eyes
spikes for nipples
and nunchucks I can work
with my buttcheeks

in my other life
I am such a lowdown filthy slut
L7 kicked me out of the band
Bratmobile kicked me
out of the band
Courtney Love is grossed out
by my hair and makeup
and Madonna is stealing my shit
left and right

in my other life
I can eat McDonald's without throwing up
I can do poetry slams
without throwing up
I can drink tap water
without getting diarrhea
I've never had a STD

my body is basically a Maserati

in my other life
I am a Black man
with so much to say
Lady Liberty gets down on her knees
hand me the torch
the Liberty Bell cracks open wider than wide
the Mississippi Delta queen cannot wait
to kiss by beautiful
African
American ass

in my other life
I am still queer
but not
you know
queeeeeeer

in my other life
I wear tiny lace panties
turn all the boys on
oh wait
that's actually this lifetime

in my other life

I am a slick chick
who can still do the splits
I do them at rock n roll shows
in restaurants, hotels, on the street
'cause I want to make sure
everyone knows my pussy
is athletic pussy
not tired pussy
floppy pussy or ragged pussy
no, she's working pussy
she's serving
she's *Blade Runner* pussy
the Terminator's terminator
Thelma and Louise
Drew Barrymore, Magnolia Thunderpussy
Pussy Galore, Mrs. Peel, and Catherine Deneuve

oh yeah, let me say that one more time
Catherine Deneuve
forget everything I said
in my other life, I am Catherine Deneuve

I am somebody else, anyway
and I look so much better than this

in my other life
I love myself as much as
Michael said he loved me
as much as Eric said he loved me
and Greg and Mark and Carol and Diane
all my friends and lovers
all your friends and lovers
are still alive and well
this whole world's just completely different

in my other life
I talk about flesh in such a way
it becomes transparent
I talk about walls and they disappear
when I bring the void into the room
it falls like a veil
so that blissful awareness
that is who I am
and who you are
becomes so present, so immediate
so perfectly known
everyone slaps his/her forehead
and goes: god

in my other life
people have no reason to be
all bitter and cynical
poetry isn't used to get laughs
Engelbert Humperdinck never happened
the Eighties never happened
Reagan was never president
the Religious Right never learned
how to get politically active
David Bowie never went straight
Ellen DeGeneres never even had to come out
Dennis Rodman is my fuckbuddy
(thank you, God)
Regis Philbin is my sugar daddy
(Lord, what can I say? I'm on my knees!)
Matt Dillon is my most recent ex-lover
(we're still very close,
we talk all the time on the phone)

I spent one glorious night with Jackie Chan
and he always treats women
with total respect no
because he knows what it is like to receive
he knows what it's like to be filled up with love
he knows there is no real difference
between the sexes
except for the positioning of society
and I have memory under my belt
that keeps me warm
on those rare nights when I go to bed alone
I feel so alive it just about breaks my heart

independent bookstores are thriving
little coffee shops with different names
are all over the place
rock n roll is still alive and kicking
Devo still sells millions of records
The Clash never stopped making records
tv is quite challenging
my father was a nice guy (very mellow, really)
Bosnia, Rwanda, and Iran
      lovely places to visit
the people there visit here just as often
everyone everywhere is filthy rich
and hung like a horse
they all want to kiss me and hug me
and fuck me
love me and cuddle me and lick me and save me
save me from my desires
save me from my fears
save me from my reincarnation woes

in my other life
I'm you
you're me
and the galaxy spins

EGAD! MY PUSSY HURTS

by beau sia
illustrated by david choe

LOVE
Beau Sia

I think love is the most beautiful thing
in the world,
and I don't give a fuck,
because I have no original ideas.
I'm a pathetic man
whose goal is to read poetry
in order
to get women
to fall in love with him,
and you'd think I was reprimanding myself
and revealing my horrible dark side
by saying that,
but I was really saying
"women who hear this, fall in love with me, or else,"
because that's what it comes down to —
an ultimatum,
life or death,
and sure, maybe I'm being extreme,
but you walk around and tell me
that things aren't extreme,
jesus,
I've seen a man jack off to a gap window display,
so don't tell me that love isn't important.

and maybe you didn't get that series of lines,
that's OK,
most of them are subtext
designed to impress people
who know too much about art,
all you need to listen to is
the 12 percent
which contain words like "fuck,"
and "ass,"
and "ride my dongstick, you naughty schoolgirl."
because in a poem about love
we all need to know the relevant things,
because we're all looking for the complete definition of love,
if only we could open our encyclopedia britannicas
and look up love and know,
but love isn't that easy.
they say cupid loved my so-called life
and when the show was cancelled
cupid cried and cried and cried and
decided that he was going to fuck up
all of humanity,
and this is why china has a trouble with its birthrate
and arkansas rhymes with date rape
and iraq is iraq,
and the fat lipo-sucked out of california
could be
its own island.

Happiness.

but this isn't a poem about geography,
this is a poem about love,
the bane of my existence,
the reason why I hate valentine's day
and halloween,
which is about ghosts
and I think you know where I'm going here.
I'm going to the land of girlfriends of halloweens past,
and maybe I've only got three ghosts in this land,
but this doesn't mean that they don't bring their friends
who are the ghosts of girls who have rejected me,
because girls rarely travel alone in this land
lydia is from this land.
I used to kiss her
while listening to
the cure's "just like heaven,"
now I don't see her anymore,
so that song makes me sad,
why must we associate music with
our love lives?
I'm not trying to be profound here,
I'm just saying that music really takes me
back, way back,
and I can't explain the memory process involved in that,
because I am not a psychology major,

and maybe
my problem with picking up women
has to do with me always asking,
"what's your major?"
but that only makes me as cheesy
as 90 percent of guys
looking for women,
and 86 percent of them have women,
so what's the deal here?
maybe I shouldn't think of women in terms
of picking them up,
and maybe I should open up my sensitive side,
but really,
the sensitive side sucks.
I've been there.
you can only imagine the kinds of sweaters
they make you wear.
it's not fair,
love is not fair,
and war is not fair,
and I don't care what anyone has to say about
any of that,
I feel unloved,
I'm sorry I need people
to tell me I'm cool,
I'm just that way.
aren't you?
am I the only one?

I know that I can't be that
misunderstood.
but you don't want to
understand me!
you just want to hear the part
where I talk about my small dick again,
because the asian man will always be plagued
by this rumor
until he is brave enough to fling it out
and say,
"HA! WE ARE GIGANTIC!"
this is not the direction
I wanted to take
this poem.
honestly, I just want to be in the arms
of my true love, in a house, in a room,
in a wonderful, perfect world with our
two children,
a boy and a girl,
helga and lamar,
but maybe I shouldn't have said this,
woody allen taught us
that marriage is a death trap.

I'm almost as old as his girlfriend.
she could be the long lost sister
I've been looking for,
maybe my mother gave her away
when we lived in china,
wait, I never lived in china.
I think I've begun lying in this poem.
I was hoping to talk about love
for 3.4 minutes
and then
come to a conclusion,
somehow defining love
within the poem,
but
I don't have any answers
and I'm looking for help from anyone,
because love has got me fucked up
and dying,
because I feel retarded without anyone to hold me,
and maybe that's sentimental,
but what's wrong with sentimental?
I just need love—
to self: fuck you, I'm OK!
you see, I can't even decide what I need
much less understand what I'm saying.
you see, all I'm saying
is
someone love me.

THE NIGHT STALKER GOT MARRIED

by juliette torrez
illustrated by ivan brunetti

THE NIGHT STALKER GOT MARRIED
Juliette Torrez

The Night Stalker got married
at San Quentin.
The serial killer took a wife
and called her Mrs. Richard Ramirez.
It was true love, they said
but they never got to go to bed,
that's not allowed
for death row inmates.
She was a freelance editor,
he was convicted of torture.
I guess they had a lot to talk about.

wicked

Juliette Torrez

Illustrations by
Steve Weissman

GATHERING OF MAMMALS
Juliette Torrez

Gathering of mammals
dancing in the dust
young beauties
weird nerdies
dressed like peacocks and ravens
cigarette machine eats a dollar
go to the beer garden
and holler to get her money back
hanging out with madcaps
who sing a cappella
at the drop of a hat
renditions for an audience of one
still looking for cigarettes
nicotine drug dealer
out right now
check back later
walk a mile for a camel
and a cup of latte
kids playing ball behind the deli
old man looking for cans in the alley
shy smiles of strangers

KAPOW!